Supreme Court
Haiku

Keith Jaasma

Supreme Court Haiku
Keith Jaasma

Supreme Court Haiku logo on front cover by Miguel Herrera
Back cover photograph by Keith Jaasma

First Edition 2018

ISBN # 978-0-359-04827-4

Publisher Keith Jaasma, 6363 Woodway, Suite 1000, Houston, Texas 77057

For more information: haikumaster@SupremeCourtHaiku.com

For my wife Amy
And my kids: Ella, Henry,
And Juliana

Preface

What is a haiku?
Japanese poetry form
Learned when I was young

First five syllables
And then seven syllables
Then five once again

U.S. Supreme Court
Often writes long opinions
That could be shorter

As short as haiku?
Sometimes it works. Sometimes not
You can be the judge

Supreme Court Haiku

The Law of the Land
In Seventeen Syllables
This Is a Haiku

Marbury v. Madison (1803)

Judicial Review

Of Congressional action

Checks and balances

Martin v. Hunter's Lessee (1816)

State court construction

Concerning Federal law

SCOTUS reigns supreme

McCulloch v. Maryland (1819)

Bank of the U.S.

Necessary and Proper

State cannot tax it

Cohens v. Virginia (1821)

State criminal case

Constitutional right claimed

SCOTUS may review

Gibbons v. Ogden (1824)

New York steamboat laws

Navigation is commerce

Reserved to Congress

United States v. The Amistad (1841)

Kidnapped Africans

Revolt at sea justified

Declared to be free

Sheldon v. Sill (1850)

Congress can't narrow

Supreme Court jurisdiction

Lower courts? It can

Cooley v. Board of Wardens (1852)

Interstate commerce

If no Federal conflict

State may regulate

Ex Parte Milligan (1866)

Habeas corpus

May only be suspended

Briefly, finitely

Texas v. White (1869)

Despite Civil War

Texas never really left

The United States

Reynolds v. United States (1878)

Free Exercise Clause

Protects belief, not action

One wife is enough

Pennoyer v. Neff (1878)

First year law students

Are required to read this

For reasons unclear

A Founding Father
Second New York Governor
And First Chief Justice

Plessy v. Ferguson (1896)

Separate Car Act

No Fourteenth Amendment bar

Jim Crow laws increase

Lochner v. New York (1905)

Bakers' hour caps

Due process violation

Freedom of contract

Weeks v. United States (1912)

Searches and seizures

Fruit of the poisonous tree

Excluded from court

Schenck v. United States (1919)

Speeches against draft

A clear and present danger

Conviction upheld

Powell v. Alabama (1932)

The Scottsboro Boys

Counsel in capital case

Due process mandate

West Coast Hotel Co. v. Parrish (1937)

State minimum wage

Protecting health and safety

Fair contract limit

Erie Railroad Co. v. Tompkins (1938)

Diversity case

State law for substantive law

No Fed common law

Wickard v. Filburn (1942)

Wheat farming limits

Affect interstate commerce

Not merely local

Chaplinsky v. New Hampshire (1942)

Fighting words doctrine

Calling churches a "racket"

May support arrest

West Virginia State Board of Education v. Barnette (1943)

Pledge of Allegiance

Jehovah's Witnesses' kids

Can't be forced to say

Korematsu v. United States (1944)

Ethnic Japanese

Relocation camps upheld

During World War II

International Shoe v. Washington (1945)

Minimum contacts

Roving salesmen lived in state

Due process given

JOHN RUTLEDGE
SECOND CHIEF JUSTICE
1795

Recess appointment
Questionable sanity
Senate rejected

Youngstown Sheet & Tube Co. v. Sawyer (1952)

President can't act

Absent power from Congress

Or Constitution

Brown v. Board of Education of Topeka (1954)

Schools for black and white

Separate is not equal

Desegregation

Mapp v. Ohio (1961)

The Fourth Amendment

The exclusionary rule

Applies to state courts

Torcaso v. Watkins (1961)

No religious tests

For government employment

Establishment Clause

Engel v. Vitale (1962)

Public school students

Can't be required to pray

Church and State apart

Gideon v. Wainwright (1963)

Appointed counsel

For those who can't afford one

Sixth Amendment right

Sherbert v. Verner (1963)

Church member fired

Would not work on holy day

Can get benefits

Jacobellis v. Ohio (1964)

Stewart concurrence

"I know it when I see it"

Not pornography

Griswold v. Connecticut (1965)

Contraceptive ban

Marital privacy right

Prevents enforcement

Griffin v. California (1965)

Closing arguments

Can't argue silence means guilt

Fifth Amendment right

Miranda v. Arizona (1966)

Suspects must be warned

The right to remain silent

The right to counsel

Harper v. Virginia Board of Elections (1966)

Poll tax not allowed

Breedlove v. Suttles reversed

Equal Protection

OLIVER ELLSWORTH
THIRD CHIEF JUSTICE
1796–1800

The Third Chief Justice
His bust at the Supreme Court
Will give you nightmares

Loving v. Virginia (1967)

Mixed-race marriages

Fundamental civil right

State may not prevent

Terry v. Ohio (1968)

Stop and frisk allowed

Reasonable suspicion

Of crime and weapon

Tinker v. Des Moines Independent Community School District (1969)

Anti-war armbands

Protected symbolic speech

Student free speech rights

Walz v. Tax Commission of the City of N.Y. (1970)

State property tax

May exempt church property

No Establishment

Lemon v. Kurtzman (1971)
(The Establishment Clause "Lemon Test")

Secular purpose

Excessive entanglement?

Primary effect

New York Times Co. v. United States (1971)

Government can't stop

Newspapers from publishing

Pentagon Papers

Wisconsin v. Yoder (1972)

Three Amish students

May leave school after eighth grade

Free Exercise Clause

Flood v. Kuhn (1972)

Baseball's reserve clause

Old antitrust exemption

Flood not free to flee

Roe v. Wade (1973)

Reproductive choice

Penumbras and due process

Through trimester two

United States v. Nixon (1974)

Watergate scandal

Executive privilege

Not unqualified

Gregg v. Georgia (1976)

Capital sentence

Not cruel and unusual

Procedures outlined

Regents of the Univ. of California v. Bakke (1978)

College admissions

Affirmative action fine

Racial quotas not

John Marshall statue
Once outside the Capitol
Now inside the Court

Bob Jones University v. United States (1983)

Private Christian school

Interracial dating ban

They must pay taxes

Lynch v. Donnelly (1984)

Jesus in manger

Amongst Santa Claus and tree

Secular purpose

New Jersey v. T.L.O. (1985)

Search of student bag

Principal needs no warrant

Search reasonable

Batson v. Kentucky (1986)

Prosecutor can't

Use peremptory challenge

To exclude a race

Edwards v. Aguillard (1987)

Creationism

Contains religious tenets

Keep from public school

Texas v. Johnson (1989)

Flag burned in protest

First Amendment protection

Expressive conduct

County of Allegheny v. ACLU (1989)

Jesus in courthouse

Menorah outside by tree

Second fine, first not

Employment Division v. Smith (1990)

Religious drug use

States need not accommodate

Conduct, not belief

Barnes v. Glen Theatre, Inc. (1991)

Fully nude dancing

Expressive, but just barely

Hoosiers may ban it

Simon & Schuster v. New York State Crime Victims Board (1991)

State's "Son of Sam" law

Can't bar profits for book by

Real-life Goodfella

Planned Parenthood v. Casey (1992)

Roe v. Wade survives

No "jurisprudence of doubt"

Stare decisis

R.A.V. v. City of St. Paul (1992)

Cross-burning by teen

"Fighting-words" statute can't reach

Targeting viewpoint

Our youngest Justice
Freed Amistad Africans
Story was his name

Lee v. Weisman (1992)

Graduation prayers

Compelled religious conduct

Undue coercion

Church of Lukumi Babalu Aye v. City of Hialeah (1993)

Chicken sacrifice

City's ban targeted sect

Actions not neutral

Zobrest v. Catalina Foothills School District (1993)

Deaf in Christian school

Sign language interpreter

State may pay for one

Daubert v. Merrell Dow Pharmaceuticals (1993)

Court is gatekeeper

For expert testimony

That's based on science

Campbell v. Acuff-Rose Music, Inc. (1994)

"Oh, Pretty Woman"

2 Live Crew "parody" song

May be a fair use

United States v. Lopez (1995)

Gun Free School Zones Act

Congressional Commerce Clause

Powers exceeded

United States v. Virginia (1996)

Military school

Males-only policy void

Equal Protection

BMW of North America v. Gore (1996)

Repainted Beamer

Four million in punitives

Excessively high

Washington v. Glucksberg (1997)

Help with suicide

Not a fundamental right

States may prosecute

United States v. Balsys (1998)

Suspected Nazi

Feared prosecution abroad

Can't invoke the Fifth

Pennsylvania Dept. of Corrections v. Yesky (1998)

State prison boot camp

Inmate with high blood pressure

ADA applies

Knowles v. Iowa (1998)

A speeding ticket

Not justification for

Search of vehicle

Dred Scott decision
Unpopular with many
From the beginning

Minnesota v. Carter (1998)

Cop watched through window

Suspects filled bags of cocaine

An illegal search

Kumho Tire Co. v. Carmichael (1999)

Daubert expert rule

Is applied to engineers

And non-scientists

City of Chicago v. Morales (1999)

Ban on loitering

Offends the First Amendment

Though gangs were target

Santa Fe Independent School District v. Doe (2000)

School cannot have prayer

On stadium intercom

Before football games

Boy Scouts of America v. Dale (2000)

Boy Scouts can't be forced

To have gay adult leader

First Amendment right

Dickerson v. United States (2000)

Congress cannot use

A statute to overrule

Miranda holding

Hill v. Colorado (2000)

State may bar protests

Within one hundred feet of

Abortion clinics

Sternberg v. Colorado (2000)

State's attempt at ban

On partial-birth abortions

Must have exceptions

Bush v. Gore (2000)

Florida recount

Cannot go forward as planned

Equal Protection

PGA Tour v. Martin (2001)

Handicapped golfer

May ride golf cart between shots

ADA applies

Board of Education v. Earls (2002)

School may require

Mandatory drug testing

For student-athletes

Zelman v. Simmons-Harris (2002)

Establishment Clause

Won't stop state's voucher program

Including church schools

Roger B. Taney
His decision in Dred Scott
May be the Court's worst

Virginia v. Black (2003)

State may prosecute

Cross-burning that is designed

To intimidate

Lawrence v. Texas (2003)

Court invalidates

State anti-sodomy laws

Overrules Bowers

McConnell v. Federal Election Commission (2003)

State scholarship plan

May bar religious study

By recipients

Maryland v. Pringle (2003)

Contraband in car

Probable cause exists to

Arrest passengers

General Dynamics Land Sys. v. Cline (2004)

The ADEA

Protects those over fifty

Not younger workers

Thornton v. United States (2004)

Search of car allowed

Incident to arrest though

Driver had left car

Blakely v. Washington (2004)

Things not admitted

That support increased sentence

Jury must find facts

Rasul v. Bush (2004)

Guantanamo Bay

Foreigner captured abroad

May be heard in court

Hamdi v. Rumsfeld (2004)

Citizen detained

As enemy combatant

May challenge findings

Gonzales v. Raich (2005)

Marijuana laws

Medical use not exempt

Federal trumps state

Gonzales v. Oregon (2006)

Feds cannot stop states

From allowing doctors to

Help with suicide

Hamdan v. Rumsfeld (2006)

Guantanamo Bay

Military commissions

Offend Geneva

The Court's first portrait
From 1867
Chase Court with the Clerk

Just one year later
Mathew Brady's studio
An eight-Justice Court

Rumsfeld v. Forum for Academic and Institutional Rights (2006)

"Don't Ask, Don't Tell" Rule

Law schools that ban recruiters

Feds can deny funds

United States v. Gonzalez-Lopez (2006)

Criminal defense

Right to attorney of choice

Structural error

Morse v. Frederick (2007)

"Bong Hits 4 Jesus"

Limited rights for students

Suspension upheld

Parents Involved in Community Schools v. Seattle School District No. 1 (2007)

Racial balancing

Compelling state interest?

Not in public schools

District of Columbia v. Heller (2008)

Second Amendment

Right of individuals

Not just militias

Exxon Shipping Co. v. Baker (2008)

Exxon Valdez crash

Oil spills; Alaskans sue

Punitives too much

Ricci v. DeStrano (2009)

White firefighters

Allowed to sue New Haven

For throwing out tests

Safford Unified School District v. Redding (2009)

Students do have rights

"Reasonable suspicion"

To conduct strip search

Presley v. Georgia (2010)

Jury selection

Public wrongly excluded

Public trial right

Citizens United v. Federal Election Commission (2010)

Ads for candidates

From corporations, unions

Are protected speech

Wilkins v. Gaddy (2010)

Force against convict

May be cruel, unusual

Despite minor harm

Thaler v. Haynes (2010)

Juror demeanor

May counter Batson challenge

Though unseen by judge

The President picks
Justices with the Senate's
Advice and Consent

Hertz Corp. v. Friend (2010)

Large corporation

"Principal place of business"

State with "nerve center"

Florida v. Powell (2010)

Warning a suspect

"Right to talk to a lawyer"

Jibes with Miranda

Berghuis v. Smith (2010)

Quite white jury pool

No Sixth Amendment issue

In quite white county

Padilla v. Kentucky (2010)

Failure to inform

Deportation risk from plea

Bad job, counselor

Stevens v. United States (2010)

Animal cruelty

Statute forbids portrayal

Overbroad on face

Stolt-Nielsen S.A. v. Animalfeeds International Corp. (2010)

Parties can't be forced

Into class arbitration

Without their consent

Johnson v. United States (2010)

"Three strikes" sentencing

Non-violent battery

Cannot be one strike

Renico v. Lett (2010)

Double Jeopardy?

Not when defendant retried

After hung jury

Graham v. Florida (2010)

Life without parole

Non-violent juvenile

Cruel, unusual

United States v. Comstock (2010)

Federal inmate

May be detained past sentence

If mentally ill

American Needle, Inc. v.
National Football League (2010)

All NFL teams

Aren't a single entity

Antitrust applies

United States v. O'Brien (2010)

Gun a machine gun?

A question for the jury

Not at sentencing

John Marshall Harlan
And John Marshall Harlan II
Both were Justices

Berghuis v. Thompkins (2010)

Miranda Rights read

Suspect silent for hours

Could waive rights later

Levin v. Commerce Energy, Inc. (2010)

Challenge to state tax

Must first be brought in state court

Comity Doctrine

Carr v. United States (2010)

Sex offender act

State lines crossed before passage

Law does not apply

Carachuri-Rosendo v. Holder (2010)

Legal resident

Second drug misdemeanor

No deportation

Holder v. Humanitarian Law Project (2010)

Law prohibiting

Support for terrorist groups

No free speech issues

Stop the Beach Renourishment v. Florida Department of Environmental Protection (2010)

Beachfront property

Cut off by restoration

Is not a taking

City of Ontario v. Quon (2010)

Cops issued pagers

Transcripts reviewed for misuse

Reasonable search

Rent-A-Center, West, Inc. v. Jackson (2010)

Arbitration clause

Agreement enforceable?

Ask arbitrator

Skilling v. United States (2010)

Houston venue fair

"Honest-services" not vague

Covers bribes, kickbacks

Doe v. Reed (2010)

State referendum

Disclosure of signatures

No free speech problem

McDonald v. Chicago (2010)

Second Amendment

Self-defense a basic right

States can't ban handguns

Christian Legal Society v. Martinez (2010)

Law school need not fund

School clubs that discriminate

Against certain groups

1886
The Waite Court was divided
On which way to look

1899
Chief Justice Melville Fuller
Twain doppelganger

Abbott v. United States (2010)

Drugs or violence

Five years added to sentence

When gun is carried

Mayo Foundation for Medical Education and Research v. United States (2011)

Doctor residents

Employees, not just students

FICA taxes due

NASA v. Nelson (2011)

NASA background check

Government as employer

Can ask drug questions

Ortiz v. Jordan (2011)

After full trial

Denied summary judgment

May not be appealed

Snyder v. Phelps (2011)

Church so full of hate

Pickets soldiers' funerals

Protected discourse

Staub v. Proctor Hospital (2011)

Reservist fired

Middle managers' actions

Can give rise to claim

Kasten v. Saint-Gobain Performance Plastics Corp. (2011)

Retaliation

Term "filed any complaint"

Includes oral claims

Arizona Christian School Tuition Organization v. Winn (2011)

Church school scholarships

Arizona tax credits

No taxpayer suits

Kentucky v. King (2011)

A warrantless search

Drug scent, sounds of destruction

Might be exigent

Brown v. Plata (2011)

Overcrowded jails

Poor medical and psych care

Set prisoners free

Chamber of Commerce of the U.S.A. v. Whiting (2011)

Immigration laws

Arizona penalties

No Fed preemption

Ashcroft v. Al-Kidd (2011)

Terrorist suspect

Warrant validates arrest

Motive matters not

Taft made him the Chief
Later Taft succeeded him
Edward Douglas White

William Howard Taft
Twenty-seventh President
Here the Chief Justice

Global Tech Appliances v. SEB S.A. (2011)

Patented fryers

Willful blindness can reflect

Induced infringement

McNeill v. United States (2011)

Three strikes sentencing

Seriousness determined

At time of priors

Microsoft v. I4I Ltd. Partnership (2011)

Patent invalid?

Defendant's standard of proof:

Clear and convincing

Sykes v. United States (2011)

Flight from cops in car

A violent felony

Three strikes law applies

J.D.B. v. North Carolina (2011)

Miranda warning

Was suspect in custody?

Child's age matters

Wal-Mart Stores, Inc. v. Dukes (2011)

Female employees

Claims lack commonality

Can't certify class

American Electric Power Co. v. Connecticut (2011)

Greenhouse gas lawsuit

No Federal common law

EPA preempts

Turner v. Rogers (2011)

The right to counsel

Applies to civil contempt

Long jail time in play

Bullcoming v. New Mexico (2011)

Confrontation Clause

Covers B.A.C. report

Testimonial

Stern v. Marshall (2011)

Anna Nicole case

Tortious interference claim

Not bankruptcy court

Brown v. Entertainment Merchants Ass'n (2011)

Ban on sales to kids

Violent video games

Fails strict scrutiny

Free Enterprise Club's Freedom Club PAC v. Bennett (2011)

Campaign matching funds

Caused by opponent spending

Burden on free speech

Louis D. Brandeis
Famous public advocate
First Jewish Justice

Goodyear Dunlop Tire v. Brown (2011)

Accident abroad

Foreign tire companies

Cannot be sued here

Golan v. Holder (2012)

Congress may expand

Copyright coverage to

Public domain works

Mims v. Arrow Financial, LLC (2012)

Robocaller suits

Can be brought in many courts

State or Federal

United States v. Jones (2012)

GPS on car

Cops installed and monitored

"Search" that needs warrant

National Meat Association v. Harris (2012)

Pig slaughterhouses

Federal regulations

Preempt state statutes

Ryburn v. Huff (2012)

School shooting rumor

Qualified immunity

Cops who entered house

Howes v. Fields (2012)

Questioned in prison

Told he could return to cell

No Miranda need

Mayo Collaborative Services v. Prometheus Laboratories (2012)

Disease treatment plan

Natural phenomena

Not patentable

Setser v. United States (2012)

Federal sentence

May run consecutive to

Future state sentence

Florence v. Board of Chosen Freeholders (2012)

Minor offenders

May be subject to strip search

Before jail entry

Mohamad v. Palestinian Authority (2012)

Torture Victim claims

Against organizations?

No, just real people

Astrue v. Capato (2012)

In vitro babies

No survivor benefits

Conceived post-mortem

The Court heard cases
Before 1935
In the Capitol

Holder v. Martinez-Gutierrez (2012)

Deportation law

Parent's time as resident

Doesn't help out child

Williams v. Illinois (2012)

DNA testing

Experts may speak of results

That others obtained

F.C.C. v. Fox Television Stations (2012)

Stray f-bombs, bare skin

Broadcast indecency rules

Fair notice lacking

Arizona v. United States (2012)

State alien law

Status confirmation fine

Three other parts not

Miller v. Alabama (2012)

Killers at fourteen

Lifetime sentence, no parole

Cruel, unusual

National Federation of Independent Business v. Sebelius (2012)

Commerce Clause can't save

Individual mandate

But Taxing Clause does

United States v. Alvarez (2012)

Stolen Valor Act

Content-based speech restriction

Fails strict scrutiny

Lozman v. City of Riviera Beach, Florida (2013)

Motorless houseboat

Outside admiralty scope

It's not a vessel

Florida v. Harris (2013)

Drug-sniffing canine

Performance log not needed

For probable cause

Gunn v. Minton (2013)

Malpractice action

Based on work on patent case

Can sue in state court

Evans v. Michigan (2013)

Double Jeopardy

Applies to man acquitted

Based on court error

Kirtsaeng v. John Wiley & Sons, Inc. (2013)

The "first sale" doctrine

Allows resale in U.S.

Books bought in Thailand

Old Senate Chamber
For some seventy-five years
The Supreme Court's home

Florida v. Jardines (2013)

Drug-sniffing dog used

A front porch is curtilage

Evidence suppressed

Marshall v. Rodgers (2013)

Waived counsel three times

No clear Sixth Amendment right

To one more lawyer

Missouri v. McNeely (2013)

D.U.I. arrest

Cops need warrant for blood test

Sans exigency

Kiobel v. Royal Dutch Petroleum Co. (2013)

Alien Tort law

Does not reach to foreign lands

Just U.S., pirates

Moncrieffe v. Holder (2013)

Immigrant's drug crime

"Aggravated felony"?

No, just a few joints

Bowman v. Monsanto Co. (2013)

Patent exhaustion

Does not give farmer the right

To replant soybeans

Maryland v. King (2013)

Serious offense

Cheek swab for DNA test

Reasonable search

Peugh v. United States (2013)

Ex Post Facto Clause

Covers Sentencing Guidelines

When range is increased

Association for Molecular Pathology v. Myriad Genetics (2013)

Can you patent it?

A DNA sequence, no

CDNA, yes

United States v. Davila (2013)

Need not vacate plea

Despite judge's involvement

When no prejudice

Salinas v. Texas (2013)

Failure to answer

Before Miranda invoked

May use at trial

Alleyene v. United States (2013)

Facts that will increase

Mandatory minimums

A jury must find

Supreme Court Building
Taft pushed for its construction
Did not live to see

Arizona v. Inter Tribal Council of Arizona (2013)

State can't require

For Federal elections

Extra documents

Agency for International Development v. Alliance for Open Society International (2013)

Tying AIDS funds to

Prostitution policy

Violates Free Speech

Fisher v. University of Texas at Austin (2013)

Race in admissions

Strict scrutiny required

Good faith not enough

Shelby County, Alabama v. Holder (2013)

"Decades-old data"

Can't justify "preclearance"

In Voting Rights Act

United States v. Windsor (2013)

States define "marriage"

Feds can't refuse to accept

A same-sex union

Stanton v. Sims (2013)

Owner hurt by gate

Qualified immunity

For cop who kicked it

Atlantic Marine Construction Co. v. United States District Court for the Western Dist. of Texas (2013)

Parties' agreement

Should usually control

Venue for lawsuit

Kansas v. Cheever (2013)

Meth-head shot sheriff

Ordered psych test can rebut

Mens rea defense

Daimler AG v. Bauman (2013)

No jurisdiction

Over foreign car maker

Based on sub's contacts

Burrage v. United States (2014)

Dealer's heroin

Must be "but for" cause of death

For enhanced sentence

Hinton v. Alabama (2014)

Counsel deficient

Failed to seek enough funds for

Strong bullet expert

Fernandez v. California (2014)

One occupant gone

Police may search residence

With other's consent

Left of the front stairs
"Contemplation of Justice"
By James Earle Fraser

Chadbourne & Parke LLP v. Troice (2014)

Stanford Ponzi scheme

Uncovered securities

State law claims allowed

United States v. Appel (2014)

Air Force base includes

Easements, protest area

Power to exclude

Lawson v. FMR LLC (2014)

Whistleblower laws

Can reach private contractors

Through Sarbanes-Oxley

Rosemond v. United States (2014)

Aiding, abetting

Use of gun during drug crime

Must know friend had gun

United States v. Castleman (2014)

Prior conviction

For domestic violence

You can't own a gun

McCutcheon v. Federal Election Commission (2014)

Aggregate limits

On campaign contributions

Violate Free Speech

Schuette v. Coalition to Defend Affirmative Action (2014)

Voters may outlaw

Use of race in admissions

At state colleges

Prado Navarette v. California (2014)

9-1-1 tipster

Gave basis for cops to stop

Pot-filled pickup truck

Town of Greece, New York v. Galloway (2014)

Establishment Clause

No sectarian prayer bar

Before town meeting

Petrella v. Metro-Goldwyn Mayer (2014)

Heir's copyright claim

Against Raging Bull movie

No laches defense

Hall v. Florida (2014)

Strict I.Q. cutoff

For capital punishment

Cruel, unusual

Plumhoff v. Rickard (2014)

High-speed police chase

Driver and passenger shot

Force not excessive

Right of the front stairs
Sits "Authority of Law"
Also by Fraser

Wood v. Moss (2014)

Bush protestors moved

Qualified immunity

For Secret Service

Martinez v. Illinois (2014)

Jeopardy attached

Although State was not ready

When jury was sworn

POM Wonderful LLC v. Coca-Cola Co. (2014)

Pomegranate juice

Lanham Act claim not barred by

Food labeling rules

Abramski v. United States (2014)

Bought gun for uncle

Punishable misstatement

Said gun was for self

Lane v. Franks (2014)

Public employee

First Amendment protection

Non-job-duty speech

American Broadcasting Cos. v. Aereo, Inc. (2014)

Web-based streaming site

Publicly performs programs

Copyrights infringed

Riley v. California (2014)

More often than not

Police will need a warrant

To search a cell phone

NLRB v. Noel Canning (2014)

Recess appointments

Intra-session included

Three days is too short

McCullen v. Coakley (2014)

Clinic buffer zone

More burdensome than needed

Violates Free Speech

Burwell v. Hobby Lobby Stores, Inc. (2014)

Birth control mandate

Corporations are "persons"

Religion burdened

Johnson v. City of Shelby (2014)

Complaint need not cite

Section 1983

For due process claim

Wagner v. Shavers (2014)

Can't use statements from

Jury deliberations

To challenge verdict

This majestic hall
Lined with busts of Justices
Leads to the Courtroom

This is a model
Of the inside of the Court
As photos are barred

Heien v. North Carolina (2014)

Officer's mistake

About state's car brake-light law

Supports traffic stop

Holt v. Hobbs (2015)

Fear of contraband

Can't stop Muslim prisoner

From having short beard

Yates v. United States (2015)

Undersized grouper

Are not tangible objects

For Sarbanes-Oxley

North Carolina Board of Dental Examiners v. Federal Trade Commission (2015)

Tar Heel State dentists

Can be sued for restrictions

On teeth whitening

Alabama Legislative Black Caucus v. Alabama (2015)

Courts must analyze

Racial gerrymandering

On district level

Young v. United Parcel Service, Inc. (2015)

Pregnant truck driver

May need accommodation

Like those disabled

Grady v. North Carolina (2015)

Ankle monitor

On sex-crime recidivist

Constitutes a search

Rodriguez v. United States (2015)

Dog sniff around car

Unreasonable seizure

When traffic stop done

Williams-Yulee v. Florida Bar (2015)

States may prohibit

Direct requests for money

From those seeking bench

Henderson v. United States (2015)

Convicted felon

May ask court to transfer guns

To gun dealer, friend

Elonis v. United States (2015)

Graphic Facebook posts

Crime if poster knew others

Would view as a threat

Zivotofsky v. Kerry (2015)

Jerusalem-born

Congress can't make passport say

Born in Israel

Hughes Court's resistance
To New Deal nearly led to
The Court-packing plan

Poor Chief Justice Stone
Died from a brain hemorrhage
Incurred on the bench

Kerry v. Din (2015)

Former Taliban

Wife can't fight denied visa

Lacks due process claim

Walker v. Texas Division, Sons of Confederate Veterans, Inc. (2015)

Confederates' Sons

Don't have right to license plate

It's government speech

Reed v. Town of Gilbert, Arizona (2015)

Content-based sign code

Fails strict scrutiny review

Can't stop large church sign

Kimble v. Marvel Entertainment, LLC (2015)

Spider-Man toy tech

License can't extend beyond

Life of the patent

City of Los Angeles, California v. Patel (2015)

Hotel guest ledgers

L.A. law lets cops inspect

Facially too broad

Horne v. Department of Agriculture (2015)

Just compensation

For personal property

Under Takings Clause

King v. Burwell (2015)

Under ACA

States with Federal Exchange

Tax credits allowed

Obergefell v. Hodges (2015)

Same-sex marriages

Must be allowed by all states

Fourteenth Amendment

Glossip v. Gross (2015)

Three-drug protocol

Fine for state's executions

No alternatives

OBB Personenverkehr AG v. Sachs (2015)

Hurt in Austria

State-owned railroad is immune

From suit in U.S.

Hurst v. Florida (2016)

Jury's decision

May not be advisory

On death penalty

Musacchio v. United States (2016)

Defendant can't raise

Statute of limitations

First time on appeal

Chief Justice Vinson
Last Chief Justice appointed
By a Democrat

Sweeping social change
Became the reputation
Of the Warren Court

V.L. v. E.L. (2016)

Full Faith and Credit

Same-sex couple's adoption

State must recognize

Wearry v. Cain (2016)

State failed to disclose

Evidence of innocence

Offends due process

Caetano v. Massachusetts (2016)

Second Amendment

Protects stun gun possession

Although it's modern

Evenwel v. Abbott (2016)

"One-person, one-vote"

Is based on population

Not those who can vote

Bank Markazi v. Peterson (2016)

Victims of terror

Can access assets held by

Iranian bank

Heffernan v. City of Paterson (2016)

Cop was demoted

For holding candidate's sign

Might have Free Speech claim

Spokeo, Inc. v. Robbins (2016)

Concrete injury

Needed to bring claim against

People search engine

Betterman v. Montana (2016)

Speedy Trial Clause

Won't stop delayed sentencing

After conviction

Wittman v. Personhuballah (2016)

Members of Congress

Can't challenge gerrymander

When not their district

Lynch v. Arizona (2016)

Life without parole

Only option besides death

Jury must be told

Commonwealth of Puerto Rico v. Sanchez Valle (2016)

U.S. and P.R.

Not separate sovereigns

Double Jeopardy

Williams v. Pennsylvania (2016)

Ex-prosecutor

Must recuse himself as judge

In appeal of case

It's Thurgood Marshall
The day he was appointed
To the Supreme Court

Dietz v. Bouldin (2016)

Inherent power

For court to recall jury

After their discharge

Taylor v. United States (2016)

Hobbs Act robbery

"Commerce" requirement met

When drug dealer robbed

Birchfield v. North Dakota (2016)

You can be punished

For refusing a breath test

Blood test? Not so much

Fisher v. University of Texas at Austin (2016)

Oh, it's you again.

UT's plan passes muster

Again. We mean it

Voisine v. United States (2016)

Domestic assault

Recklessness based conviction

No gun possession

Bosse v. Oklahoma (2016)

Victim's family

Cannot recommend sentence

Per Eighth Amendment

Salman v. United States (2016)

Insider trading

Tipper to friends, family

Need not reap profit

Buck v. Davis (2017)

Letting expert say

That race predicts violence

Is bad lawyering

Pena-Rodriguez v. Colorado (2017)

No-impeachment rule

Must yield to Sixth Amendment

When juror's racist

Manuel v. Joliet (2017)

Plaintiff may challenge

His pretrial detention

With Fourth Amendment

Star Athletica, LLC v. Varsity Brands, Inc. (2017)

Copyright protects

Uniform surface design

Not shape, cut, or size

Moore v. Texas (2017)

I.Q. scores alone

Don't determine fitness for

The death penalty

At this point in time
The Court had five members with
Cool hipster glasses

The nine Justices
Who decided Bush v. Gore
And an election

Goodyear Tire & Rubber v. Haeger (2017)

Litigant's bad faith

Court may award only fees

Caused by misconduct

Nelson v. Colorado (2017)

Due process mandates

Restitution's return when

Conviction reversed

Cooper v. Harris (2017)

State may not use race

As predominant factor

In drawing districts

TC Heartland v. Kraft Food Group Brands (2017)

Patent venue fight

Corporation resides where

Incorporated

Session v. Morales-Santana (2017)

Children born abroad

Must treat moms and dads the same

For citizenship

Matal v. Tam (2017)

"The Slants" trademark barred

Viewpoint discrimination

Band can register

Packingham v. North Carolina (2017)

Social media

State can't bar sex offender

From all types of use

Trinity Lutheran v. Comer (2017)

Church school has playground

Free Exercise Clause gives it

Access to state grant

Pavan v. Smith (2017)

Birth certificates

Child of same-sex spouses

Both must be listed

Dunn v. Madison (2017)

Memory of crime

Is not a requirement

For death penalty

District of Columbia v. Wesby (2018)

Vacant house party

Unlawful entry arrests

Probable cause found

Jennings v. Rodriguez (2018)

Detained alien

No statutory bond right

Pending decision

Beyond this curtain
Starting October each year
Oral arguments

Jesner v. Arab Bank, PLC (2018)

Victims cannot use

Alien Tort Statute to

Sue corporation

Murphy v. NCAA (2018)

Federal ban on

State-permitted sports gambling

Barred commandeering

Byrd v. United States (2018)

Vehicle driver

May expect some privacy

Though not the renter

McCoy v. United States (2018)

When your client wants

To insist he's not guilty

You have to let him

Epic Systems Corp. v. Lewis (2018)

NLRA won't

Stop solo arbitration

If parties agreed

Collins v. Virginia (2018)

No vehicle search

In curtilage of a home

Without a warrant

Minnesota Voters Alliance v. Mansky (2018)

Polling place ban on

Political apparel

Offends Free Speech Clause

South Dakota v. Wayfair, Inc. (2018)

States can charge sales tax

To large out-of-state shippers

Quill case overruled

Carpenter v. United States (2018)

Cell-site records grab

Is a Fourth Amendment search

Likely need warrant

Currier v. Virginia (2018)

Double Jeopardy?

Not when defendant consents

To second trial

Abbott v. Perez (2018)

Districts in Texas

Taint of discrimination?

Burden on plaintiff

Janus v. American Federation of State, County, and Municipal Employees (2018)

State can't take fees from

Public employees who shun

Union membership

Women Justices
O'Connor, Sotomayor,
Ginsburg, and Kagan

Roberts Court today
Except Justice Kennedy
He has retired

Trump v. Hawaii (2018)

Latest travel ban

Within discretion granted

To the President

NIFLA v. Becerra (2018)

Pregnancy centers

Probably can't be forced to

Discuss abortion

Masterpiece Cakeshop v. Colorado Civil Rights Commission (2018)

Commission can't be

Hostile toward Christian baker's

Sincere faith-based views

OR

Free Exercise Clause

Baker won't be forced to bake

Same-sex wedding cake

We have reached the end

Or is it the beginning?

No. It is the end.

Photograph Credits

Pages 5, 41, 61, 69, 101– Keith Jaasma ("Author").

Page 9 – Author photograph of bust of John Jay, by Bruce Hoheb and Vincenzo Polumbo after John Frazee (1978), Collection of the Supreme Court of the United States.

Page 13 – Author photograph of bust of John Rutledge, by Bruce Hoheb (1976), Collection of the Supreme Court of the United States.

Page 17 – Author photograph of bust of Oliver Ellsworth, by Bruce Hoheb (1976), Collection of the Supreme Court of the United States.

Page 21 – Author photograph of John Marshall statute, sculpted by William Wetmore Story (1883).

Page 25 – Author photograph of "Joseph Story" by G.P.A. Healey (1813-1894), Collection of the Supreme Court of the United States.

Page 29 – a. Drawing of Dred Scott from Frank Leslie's Illustrated Newspaper, June 27, 1857. b. Author photograph of historical poster. Both from the Collection of the United States Capitol.

Page 33 – Author photograph of bust of Roger B. Taney, by Horatio Stone (circa 1854), Collection of the Supreme Court of the United States.

Page 37 – a. The Chase Court, (February 1867), by Alexander Gardner. b. The Chase Court, (March-April 1868), by Mathew Brady. Both from the Collection of the Supreme Court of the United States.

Page 45 – a. John Marshall Harlan, Library of Congress, Brady-Hand Collection. b. John Marshall Harlan II, Collection of the Supreme Court of the United States.

Page 49 – a. The Waite Court (February 1886), George Prince b. The Fuller Court, (May 1899), the C.M. Bell Studio. Both from the Collection of the Supreme Court of the United States.

Page 53 – a. The White Court (October 1916), Clinedinst Studio. Collection of the Supreme Court of the United States. b. The Taft Court, Harris & Ewing, Inc., Donated to the Library of Congress, 1955.

Page 57 – Louis Brandeis (circa 1916), Library of Congress.

Page 65 – Collection of the Architect of the Capitol.

Page 73 – Author photograph of "Contemplation of Justice" by James Earle Fraser (1935).

Page 77 – Author photograph of "Authority of Law" by James Earle Fraser (1935).

Page 81 – a. The Author b. Author photograph of model from the Collection of the Supreme Court of the United States.

Page 85 – a. Hughes Court, Library of Congress. B. Author photograph of bust of Harlan Fiske Stone, by (Percy) Bryant Baker (circa 1952), Collection of the Supreme Court of the United States.

Page 89 – a. Photograph of Vinson Court. b. Photograph of Warren Court. Both from Collection of the Supreme Court of the United States.

Page 93 – Photograph of Thurgood Marshall (1967), National Archives.

Page 97 – a. Photograph of Burger Court. b. Photograph of Rehnquist Court. Both from Collection of the Supreme Court of the United States.

Page 105 – a. Photograph of Roberts Court, Collection of the Supreme Court of the United States b. Photograph of Justices O'Connor, Sotomayor, Ginsburg, and Kagan. Steve Petteway, Collection of the Supreme Court of the United States.

About the Poet

Keith is a lawyer

He lives with his wife and kids

Near Houston, Texas

Twitter: @supremehaiku
Facebook: @supremecourthaiku

SupremeCourtHaiku.com
SupremeCourtHaiku.net
haikumaster@supremecourthaiku.com

Merchandise: https://www.zazzle.com/kjaasma

www.ingramcontent.com/pod-product-compliance
Lightning Source LLC
Chambersburg PA
CBHW030848180526
45163CB00004B/1493